When your CRUSH Isn't CRUSHING

Overwhelming or Hurting, you'll be fine.

By
CYNTHIA LEONARD

TABLE OF CONTENTS

Both you and I are helpless against it. Going through the feelings may be quite draining at times, particularly if your crush is unaware of you or your existence. Therefore, all you can do is wait until you decide to "Brave up" one day.

Is the answer "Yea" or "Nah"?

WHAT'S A CRUSH AND HOW DOES IT FEEL?

Having a crush usually means that you have intensely amorous or enamoured emotions for someone. It is often characterised by an intense attraction to and interest in another person, generally someone you know or have met. When you develop feelings for someone, you can find yourself thinking about them often and wishing you could see them more often.

Having a crush might feel different for every person, but it often includes a mix of excitement, trepidation, and stomach butterflies. When you're near your crush or even simply thinking about them, you could experience heightened enjoyment and anticipation. Your pulse rate may go up and you could find yourself thinking about romantic situations or having fantasies about getting together with them.

Crushes may be thrilling as well as frightening. On the one hand, they could make you feel happy and a surge of good feelings. On the other hand, they may also be accompanied with apprehension and confusion, particularly if you're unclear if your crush feels the same way about you.

Being exposed to the prospect of rejection or unrequited love makes having a crush on someone make you feel somewhat vulnerable.

Developing a crush may be a thrilling and very emotional process. As you work through your emotions for someone you're attracted to, it might bring a combination of joy, excitement, worry and even a little amount of vulnerability.

HOW CRUSHES HAPPEN AND COMMON EXPERIENCES

Having a crush: This is the first sign that you are beginning to have emotions for someone. Finding someone appealing, being intrigued by their demeanour or having a connection with them are frequent components.

Butterflies in the stomach: You could feel butterflies in the pit of your stomach when you see or engage with your crush. The thrill or anxiety that comes with being with someone you have emotions for causes what is popularly referred to as "butterflies in the stomach" to appear.

Constantly thinking about them: When your crush isn't there, it's normal to daydream or fantasise about them. Crushes often fill your thoughts. All day long, they can be on your thoughts, making it challenging to concentrate on anything else.

Increase heart rate and nervousness: Your pulse rate may speed and you may get uneasy or apprehensive when you're close or in the company of your crush. This is a physical reaction to the thrill or anticipation of being with someone you find attractive.

Difficulty acting natural or speaking: Speaking or behaving normally is difficult when your crush is present. Many individuals find it difficult to act themselves or participate in casual conversation. This may include verbal stuttering, feelings of awkwardness, or even a complete avoidance of social contacts.

Seeking their affirmation and attention: It's normal to want your crush's attention or validation. It's possible that you'll find yourself attempting to win their favour, looking for chances to be in their presence, or paying more attention to your behaviour and appearance while they're around.

Jealousy: Feelings of jealousy might surface when your crush pays attention to someone else or when someone else shows interest in you. This is a common reaction to a possessive attachment or worry about losing their attention.

Reading too much into tiny acts or exchanges: If you have a crush on someone, you can find yourself overanalyzing every exchange. Even while they may not really mean as much, little gestures, compliments, and even cursory chats can be regarded as meaningful indications of interest.

Sharing with friends: Friends often talk about their crushes. You could find yourself talking about your infatuation with close friends, asking them for help, or just raving over them.

Crushes may be an emotional rollercoaster that is filled with uncertainty. One second you could be joyful and full of optimism, and the next you might be dejected or unhappy. These emotional ups and downs may be influenced by your uncertainty over the other person's sentiments towards you.

ROLE OF ATTRACTION AND INFATUATION

Two emotional states known as attraction and infatuation often take place in the context of romantic partnerships or close interpersonal bonds. Even while they have certain things in common, they also have unique traits and duties.

In general, the term "attraction" describes the sensation of being pulled to someone or something. It may appear as physical, emotional, intellectual or sexual attraction, among other manifestations. While emotional attraction is linked to a strong emotional connection, physical attraction is often focused on how someone looks. While sexual attraction entails a strong need for intimacy and physical contact, intellectual attraction may be triggered by common interests or intriguing talks.

Relationship initiation and formation are significantly influenced by attraction. It operates as a catalyst to bring individuals together, builds a base for future inquiry and connection, and inspires the pursuit of romantic engagement. Mutual attraction makes people more inclined to look for chances to communicate and spend time and effort getting to know one another.

However, infatuation is characterised by a strong, ardent and even obsessive concern with the object of one's affection. Idealising the other person and having a strong desire to be with them are involved. Short-lived infatuation often stems from imagination and projection rather than a thorough comprehension of the other person's genuine nature.

Early on in a love relationship, infatuation may be present. It may elicit feelings of excitement, stomach butterflies, and heightened emotions. It's crucial to understand that infatuation is not a solid basis for a long-lasting, healthy relationship. It is a transient condition that might impair judgement and make it challenging to perceive the other person objectively.

A deeper and more mature type of love, characterised by sincere concern, respect and emotional connection, often replaces infatuation with time. It's critical to get beyond infatuation and have a better understanding of each other's beliefs, aspirations and compatibility as a relationship develops.

Do know that both attraction and infatuation have significant effects on romantic relationships. Infatuation may increase intensity and excitement in the early phases, while attraction acts as the first spark that attracts individuals together. However, a relationship must go beyond infatuation and build true love, trust and compatibility in order to succeed.

IS IT WRONG TO HAVE A CRUSH?

No, having a crush is OK. It's normal and usual for many individuals to experience having a crush. It is a typical aspect of human attraction and emotions. Finding someone intriguing, attractive or compatible in any other manner triggers a natural reaction of developing affections for them. It may be a fun and thrilling experience.

However, it's critical to comprehend the restrictions and requirements that come with having a crush. Respecting the other person's individuality and sentiments is crucial. It's also important to understand that just because you have emotions for someone, it doesn't mean you have to go into a romantic relationship with them. Approaching the problem with respect, understanding and open dialogue is crucial.

When a crush causes intrusive or obsessive thoughts, interferes with your capacity to maintain healthy relationships or includes harassment or non-consensual behaviour, it becomes a problem. When handling crushes, it is essential to have a balanced viewpoint and to put everyone's safety and consent as a priority.

IMPACT OF CRUSHES ON SELF-ESTEEM AND SELF-IMAGE

Crushes may have a big effect on how you feel about yourself and how you see yourself, both favourably and negatively. Let's analyse how crushes might alter these aspects:

Positive Impact:

- Boosting self-esteem: When someone develops a crush on us, it may make us feel desirable and beautiful. The attention and interest from the crush might increase our self-esteem, making us feel more confident and valued.

- Positive self-image: Being appreciated by someone we have a crush on might lead to a more positive self-image. We may perceive ourselves as deserving of love and create a more positive impression of our physical appearance, personality, and characteristics.

Negative Impact:

Crushes may sometimes cause people to feel uneasy about themselves. They could judge themselves by the crush's idealised norms, which might leave them feeling inadequate or self-conscious.

- Self-consciousness: When someone has a crush on us, we may become more self-conscious about our actions, appearance and behaviour. This heightened self-awareness may produce worry and impair our self-esteem if we believe we're not living up to the crush's expectations.

- Rejection and disappointment: When our emotions for a crush are not reciprocated, it may be detrimental to our self-esteem. Rejection may lead to emotions of worthlessness, doubting our attractiveness, and a damage to our self-image.

It's crucial to remember that the influence of crushes on self-esteem and self-image may vary based on the individual and their unique experiences. Some individuals could be more resilient and able to keep a positive self-perception, whilst others might be more negatively impacted by rejection or anxieties.

To lessen the harmful consequences of crushes, it's crucial to retain a healthy perspective and promote self-care. This involves concentrating on self-acceptance, recognizing personal value beyond romantic interests and participating in activities that enhance self-confidence and personal progress. Building a strong support network of friends and family who can provide emotional support can also be beneficial.

TYPES OF CRUSHES

Celebrity Crushes:

Celebrity crushes have always been a curiosity for folks throughout the world. Whether it's an actress, singer, athlete, or other prominent person, the appeal and intrigue connected with celebrity crushes are apparent. This short analyses the topic of having celebrity crushes, investigating the causes for their ubiquity and the impact they may have on people.

Escape and imagination: One of the key reasons individuals develop celebrity crushes is the potential for escape and the chance to engage in imagination. Celebrities typically exemplify attributes such as beauty, skill, charm and prosperity, which may be enticing for individuals seeking a momentary getaway from their daily life. By adoring a celebrity from afar, people might project their own wants and aspirations onto these characters, producing a feeling of imagination and excitement.

Idealisation and motivation: Celebrity crushes may serve as a source of motivation, especially when it comes to personal ambitions and objectives. Many people look up to their celebrity crushes as role models, praising their successes, abilities, and charity activities. The perceived idealised image of a celebrity can motivate individuals to strive for their own personal growth and success.

Emotional Connection and Identification: The parasocial connection phenomena plays a crucial part in celebrity crushes. People may have a feeling of emotional connection with a celebrity, despite never having met them in person. The public persona of a celebrity, developed via media coverage and performances, may provoke powerful emotions and a sensation of familiarity. Fans often feel linked to their celebrity crushes via comparable hobbies, experiences, or even personal challenges, establishing a feeling of empathy and connection.

Entertainment and Pop Culture Influence: The entertainment industry and popular culture play a key part in fuelling the formation of celebrity crushes.

Through movies, music, television programmes and social media platforms, celebrities are continually in the limelight, establishing a ubiquitous presence in people's lives. The repeated exposure to these characters enhances their impact and appeal, making it simpler for individuals to form crushes and retain their interest.

Healthy Appreciation vs Obsession: While celebrity crushes may be a harmless kind of entertainment, it is crucial to keep a healthy perspective. For most people, celebrity crushes are a transient infatuation that gives delight and excitement. It's crucial to discern between adoration that is healthy and obsession, however. Obsessive behaviours, such as excessive stalking, intrusive thoughts, or ignoring real-life relationships, may be damaging to one's well-being and should be handled if they emerge.

School or Workplace Crushes:

Crushes at school or work are widespread and may often bring a little thrill and anticipation to our everyday routines. Here are some things to think about and advice for dealing with crowds in these situations:

Respect limits and preserve professionalism: It's crucial to act professionally whether you're at work or school. Keep an eye on your behaviour to make sure you don't cross any boundaries or cause any awkward circumstances.

Focus on personal development: Don't only think about your infatuation; think about how you can improve yourself. To succeed in your chosen sector, put effort into your education or employment. This not only makes you a better version of yourself but also offers chances for achievement and personal fulfilment.

Set priorities for your obligations: It's important to keep in mind that your major priorities should continue to be work or education. Don't allow your crush to cause you to neglect your obligations. To preserve your reputation and accomplish your objectives, stay on top of your duties.

Create a relationship first: Create a relationship with your crush first if you want to learn more about them. Develop a foundation of trust and understanding by striking up informal discussions, identifying shared hobbies, and more. By using this strategy, you may assess their interest and compatibility while maintaining respect and comfort.

Be aware of power dynamics: If there is a big gap in seniority or hierarchy between you and your crush, it's extremely crucial to be aware of power dynamics in the workplace. Before pursuing a love connection under such circumstances, think about the possible outcomes and repercussions.

Respect for permission and boundaries: It's critical to respect your crush's privacy and personal space. To gauge how comfortable they are, watch for verbal and nonverbal clues. Get their clear approval before making any amorous approaches since consent is crucial.

If necessary, seek advice: If you find it difficult to control your emotions or the issue grows problematic, think about asking a dependable friend, mentor, or counsellor for advice. They can assist you negotiate the complications of a crush at school or at work by offering helpful guidance and support.

Crushes are a natural part of life, but it's important to treat them delicately and with respect while keeping in mind the broader context of your academic or professional setting.

Childhood Crushes And Nostalgia:

Both nostalgia and childhood romances may stir up intense feelings and memories. Many individuals recall their first crushes with affection since they often carry these memories close to their hearts. On the other hand, nostalgia is a yearning or nostalgic attachment to the past. When thinking back on former times, it often contains a bittersweet combination of delight and melancholy.

Childhood crushes are often benign and might be seen as an early kind of adoration or obsession with a person. They often happen while kids are in elementary or middle school, when they are beginning to understand how they feel about other people. These crushes might be anything from fleeting fancies to intense, unrequited adoration.

There are many different causes for early crushes. A crush might sometimes arise from a physical appeal, but it can also be brought on by traits like compassion, humour, or ability. Daydreaming, flushing, and a want to be around the other person are frequent symptoms of a crush. Though they are more innocent and unrequited, childhood crushes differ from romantic relationships in fundamental ways.

On the other hand, nostalgia is a complicated feeling that incorporates yearning for the past. It often manifests when we reflect on happy childhood memories, occasions or events. Numerous triggers, such as specific fragrance, a song or travelling to a location with a connection to our past, might cause nostalgia.

A sense of nostalgia may be both reassuring and depressing. It enables us to relive special memories and feel the emotions connected to them. It may also help us see how we've evolved and matured through time by giving us a feeling of continuity and connection to our prior selves.

Engaging in nostalgia and youthful love may be a source of happiness and warmth as well as a chance for introspection. People often recall their first loves and the innocent, even embarrassing, situations that went along with them. Through shared experiences and an appreciation of our common memories, telling these tales to friends or loved ones may strengthen relationships.

Nostalgia and childhood loves have a particular place in many people's hearts since they signify a period of youth, exploration and happy memories. They serve as a reminder of our development and the feelings we went through while negotiating the difficulties of interpersonal relationships and moving through life.

Crushes On Friends Or Acquaintances:

Crushes on acquaintances or friends are pretty frequent, although they may sometimes be tricky to handle. It's normal to sense a connection or spend time with someone you have emotions for. But it's crucial to manage these circumstances delicately and with respect for everyone involved. Here are some things to think about:

Self-analysis: Give yourself some time to comprehend your own emotions and driving forces. Think about what it is about this individual that appeals to you and if this is a true connection or only infatuation.

Analyse the circumstance: Analyse the interactions between you and your friends or acquaintances. Consider how continuing a romantic relationship could affect your current relationship. Think about the long-term effects and if the risk is worthwhile.

Communication: It's important to be honest and open with one another. You may express your emotions to the individual involved if you're at ease. But be ready for the potential that they may not feel the same way about you. It's critical to respect their answer and refrain from pressuring them.

Maintain proper limits and show respect for the other person's choices and personal space. Recognise that, particularly if they weren't previously aware of your sentiments, they may require some time to evaluate their own feelings.

Acceptance and moving on: It's important to appreciate your crush's choice and make an effort to move on if they don't share your sentiments. It could be difficult at first, but putting your attention on other

elements of your life, doing new things and hanging out
with friends will help you refocus your emotions.

Maintaining friendships and acquaintances is crucial
since they are useful. Although it's OK to have a crush,
sustaining such relationships—whether they turn into
anything serious or not—requires treating it with
maturity and respect.

FACTORS INFLUENCING CRUSHES

Physical Appearance And Attractiveness:

In truth, physical appeal and appearance may have a big impact on crushes. The first thing that draws someone in is often their appearance. Some physical characteristics that might affect crushing include:

Face: Many individuals might find attractive face traits including symmetry, clean skin, pronounced cheekbones, and expressive eyes.

Body type: Depending on the person, they could desire a leaner physique, a muscular build, or a curvier body shape.

Height: The height of a person may also influence their attractiveness; some people may find taller persons more alluring, while others may prefer shorter ones.

Personal grooming: Maintaining good personal hygiene, dressing stylishly, and generally taking care of one's appearance may increase one's attractiveness and appeal to possible crushes.

A person's physical characteristics are often what first sparks an attraction, it's also important to understand that other factors have a role in how intense or long-lasting a crush becomes. Other elements that are important in creating and sustaining crushes include personality features, common interests, intellect, sense of humour and emotional compatibility. People may find themselves first drawn to someone based on looks, but they may become closer to them as a result of these deeper attributes.

Similarities And Shared Interests:

Similarities and same interests are undoubtedly among the elements that might have a big impact when it comes to crushes. These are some ways they may affect crushes:

Common Ground: When you learn that you have something in common with someone, it makes you feel closer and more at ease. This shared experience may help lay the groundwork for attraction and increase your level of comfort in their presence.

Emotional connection: Emotional connection often results from comparable interests and experiences. Finding someone who shares your interests or has similar opinions may help you feel understood and validated. Your emotions for the individual may get stronger and more intense as a result of this emotional connection.

Topics for Conversation: Talking about common interests is a natural progression. When you can chat about something you both appreciate, it's simpler to interact with someone. As a result, there may be more in-depth and regular exchanges, which will give the crush time to build.

Similarities and common hobbies might point to your crush and you having a certain amount of compatibility. You could think that you and the other person are on the same page and have a good chance of getting along. The crush may become more intense and appealing as a result of this impression of compatibility.

Finding someone who is compatible with your hobbies might help you feel welcomed and valued. Humans naturally want approval from others, so when someone shows appreciation for something we love, it may make us feel good. This affirmation may increase your attraction to the individual and fuel your infatuation.

Psychological Projection And Idealisation:

Idealisation and psychological projection are two psychological processes that might affect crushes. Let's go further into each of these elements:

Psychological projection is a defence strategy wherein people project their own emotions, characteristics, or ideas onto other people. Psychological projection may appear in relation to crushes in a number of ways:

Unconscious Desires: Sometimes, people fall in love with someone because they believe that person represents characteristics or features that they want but don't have. In this situation, the person may transfer their own wishes to the person they are crushing on.

Unresolved concerns might cause people to transfer their problems or unpleasant previous experiences onto their crush. For instance, if someone has previously been rejected or abandoned, they could project those concerns onto their crush and worry about being rejected once again.

Idealised Image: People could imagine what their crush should be like in an idealised way, giving them traits that may or may not be true. This projection, which is based on the person's own wishes and expectations rather than the reality of the person, may lead to an erroneous impression of the crush.

Idealisation: Idealisation is the propensity to see someone as faultless or ideal while often ignoring their defects or inadequacies. Idealisation may be quite important when it comes to crushes:

- People sometimes pay more attention to the good qualities of their crush while downplaying or disregarding any unfavourable features or behaviours. This focus on just certain things might cause one to idealise and see another as flawless.

Emotional Intensity: Crushes often cause strong feelings, and these strong emotions might lead to idealisation. The intense emotions that come with a crush may elicit exhilaration and cause someone to see their crush through rose-coloured glasses.

Daydreaming and Fantasising: People sometimes daydream or fantasise about their crush, imagining idealised situations. These fantasies might strengthen the process of idealisation and support the belief that the crush is flawless or ideal.

Social And Cultural Factors Shaping Crushes:

As a complicated and multidimensional element of human emotions, crushes are impacted by a variety of social and cultural circumstances. Here are some important elements that might influence crushes:

Social standards and Expectations: In terms of romantic relationships and attraction, society and culture often set standards and expectations. The kinds of persons that people are supposed to be drawn to or pursue as crushes might be influenced by these conventions. For instance, social expectations may place a premium on a partner's physical appearance or certain behavioural attributes, which might influence the development of crushes.

Media and Pop Culture: The media significantly influences how we see romance and beauty. In movies, television programmes, and advertisements, representations of perfect relationships, love tales, and gorgeous people may mould our crushes and impact our tastes. Crush perception may be greatly influenced by media portrayals of beauty standards, love gestures, and relationship dynamics.

Peer Influence: The emergence of crushes is significantly influenced by peers and social circles. Who a person develops a crush on might depend on their need for social acceptability and affirmation. The objects of one's attention might change depending on what their peers think, their shared interests and their friends' approval or disapproval.

Cultural Background and Values: Cultural backgrounds and values have a big impact on how crushes develop. The ideas of beauty, romance and relationship dynamics vary between countries. The targets of attachment and the methods in which crushes are pursued might be influenced by cultural views, such as the value of family approval or customs around romance.

Gender Roles and Expectations: Gender roles and expectations have a significant impact on how crushes develop. Who is deemed a suitable object of attraction might vary depending on societal ideals of masculinity and femininity. For instance, conventional gender norms may dictate that males should seek women, which may have an impact on the dynamics of courting and the development of crushes.

Personal Experiences: Crush development is influenced by personal experiences, including former relationships, familial dynamics and personal views. Previous happy or unhappy love and relationship experiences may shape the attributes people look for in a crush and have an impact on how open and vulnerable they are.

Socialisation and Upbringing: An individual's upbringing and socialisation within a certain culture or group may affect how they see love relationships and how they develop crushes. An individual's tastes and expectations towards crushes might be influenced by cultural conventions, familial beliefs and the relationship modelling they saw as children.

IS IT OK IF THE CRUSH IS NOT MUTUAL?

A one-sided or non-reciprocal crush is quite acceptable. Unrequited crushes are really quite prevalent and affect a lot of individuals at some time in their life. It might be a difficult and perhaps discouraging experience, but it's crucial to keep in mind that shared emotions cannot be pushed or controlled.

It's important to respect the other person's sentiments and limits when your infatuation isn't reciprocal. It is inappropriate to coerce or trick someone into sharing your sentiments. Instead, concentrate on comprehending and accepting the circumstances. Finding appropriate coping mechanisms for your emotions, such as chatting to friends, participating in activities or getting support from others, may be beneficial.

Know that there are a lot of other individuals out there with whom you may establish future friendships. Unrequited sentiments are common and as time passes, you can notice that your feelings change or that you meet someone else who shares your interests.

EMOTIONAL INTENSITY AND ROLLER COASTER OF FEELINGS

The thrilling and powerful feeling of having a crush is often characterised by a rollercoaster of emotions. These are some of the emotional phases that you could experience when you have a crush:

Excitation: When a crush first starts to form, it's common to feel excited. Every time you see or interact with the person you have a crush on, you can experience an adrenaline rush. There may be delight and excitement in the prospect of seeing them.

Infatuation: As your affections for the individual intensify, you could feel this way. They could dominate your thoughts, idealising their traits and making you envision a loving future with them. This obsession might cause you to fantasise a lot and concentrate more on the subject of your adoration.

Euphoria: When your crush acknowledges your emotions or expresses interest in you, it might cause you to feel ecstatic. A rush of satisfaction and joy may be brought on by mutual validation and attraction. You could feel on top of the world when your crush makes flattering comments or gestures.

Worry: Having a crush may cause worry and anxiety in addition to the good feelings. A persistent state of anxiety may be brought on by emotions of fear of rejection, ambiguity about their sentiments and worries about saying or doing the wrong thing. You can overthink every encounter and feel awkward with them.

Jealousy: Observing your crush interacting with others may make you feel envious. They could engage with other prospective love partners, which might make you possessive and feel threatened. Jealousy may intensify sentiments and cause insecurity.

Frustration might develop if your crush doesn't reciprocate your sentiments or gives out conflicting signals. You can feel emotionally drained by the ambiguity and uncertainty and want for your crush to be clear or to reciprocate you.

Heartache: Losing a crush or unrequited love may be difficult experiences. You could feel grief and despair if your emotions aren't returned or if a romantic relationship can't progress due to certain conditions. There might be extremes of deep melancholy and desire, making it seem like an emotional rollercoaster.

NERVOUSNESS, ANXIETY AND UNCERTAINTY

It's very natural to have these feelings when you're crushing someone. Since crushes sometimes entail intense feelings and the dread of rejection or the unknown, it's a typical sensation for many individuals. These are a few causes for these emotions to manifest:

Fear of Rejection: There's always a potential that someone you have a crush on won't feel the same way, or that things won't work out. This worry of being rejected might cause anxiety and apprehension about how the other person will react to your emotions.

Vulnerability: Having a crush often entails exposing oneself emotionally and leaving oneself exposed to possible harm. Being vulnerable might make you uneasy and unsure of how to handle the circumstance.

Overanalyzing: It's normal to analyse each encounter and discussion you have with your crush. As you strive to understand their behaviours or words, frequent analysis might raise tension and unease.

Lack of Control: Crushes might give you the impression that you have little influence over how things will turn out. Because you can't foresee how the other person will respond or if the connection will develop, you could experience anxiety.

Here are some suggestions for controlling these emotions:

Realise that it is typical: Remind yourself that having a crush is normal and causes you to feel apprehensive, uncomfortable, and hesitant. It's OK to have these feelings, and many other people have had similar experiences.

Put self-care first: Take part in relaxing and calming activities. Maintain your physical and mental health by engaging in leisure activities, socialising with friends, and using relaxation methods like deep breathing or mindfulness.

Take baby steps: Concentrate on forging a connection with the person you have a crush on rather than overloading yourself with ideas of a prospective relationship. Get to know them better gradually by starting with short talks.

Set realistic expectations: Recognise that it's acceptable if a crush doesn't develop into a romantic relationship. Avoid putting too much pressure on either you or the other person. Enjoy getting to know someone rather than concentrating just on the result.

Seek assistance: Discuss your emotions with close friends or family members you can trust. Sharing your worries and anxieties might help ease some of the uncertainty and fear. Additionally, if your emotions of fear or uncertainty become excessive and interfere with your regular life, think about getting professional treatment.

IMPACT ON SOCIAL INTERACTIONS AND RELATIONSHIPS

Relationships and social interactions may both be impacted by having a crush. They may be impacted in the following ways:

Focus: When you have a crush on someone, your thoughts about them often take over your head. It may be difficult to focus on other social interactions and relationships because of this sharpened attention. You could find yourself daydreaming or thinking about your crush all the time, which can make it difficult for you to interact completely with other people.

Shyness and Nervousness: Crushes may make you feel uncomfortable and uneasy, especially if the person you're attracted to is around. Social interactions may become more difficult as a result because you may feel more self-conscious or anxious about coming across positively. You could therefore be less inclined to strike up talks or participate in social activities.

Changed Behaviour: If you have a crush on someone, you could change your behaviour to impress or attract their attention. Your demeanour, style or hobbies may change as a result of being more aware of how you come across. Your current relationships may be impacted by these changes if your friends or acquaintances think you are behaving differently or putting your crush before them.

Reduced Availability: Hanging out with your sweetheart can come before other social engagements or obligations. In an effort to be close to your infatuation, you could find yourself turning down invitations or spending less time with friends and family. Existing connections may be strained by this change in availability and others may feel overlooked or unimportant.

Heightened Emotional State: Crushes often accompany powerful emotional states like excitement, pleasure or worry. These more intense emotional states may affect your general attitude and behaviour, which may have an effect on how you interact with other people. Based on the feelings you have for your crush, you can become more enthusiastic, communicative or even more quiet and introverted.

Jealousy and Insecurity: Observing your crush interacting with others or expressing interest in someone else might make you feel envious and insecure. If you compare your current romantic connections to the idealised version of your crush, these feelings may negatively impact your interactions with friends or even cause them to become strained.

Be aware of these possible effects and work towards striking a good balance between going after your love interest and sustaining crucial connections with other people. You may overcome these obstacles and make sure that your crush doesn't have a detrimental impact on your relationships and social interactions by communicating and reflecting on yourself.

COPING STRATEGIES AND RESOLUTIONS

Managing Unrequited Crushes

Unrequited crushes may be difficult and emotionally taxing to deal with. Here are some pointers for controlling your emotions in such circumstances:

Accept your emotions: Even if you don't feel the same way about someone, it's vital to recognise and accept your feelings of attraction. Recognise that you're not alone in experiencing unrequited love; it's a typical human experience.

Give yourself some time and space so that you may process your feelings and recover. While feeling disappointed, unhappy, or upset is OK, try not to wallow in these feelings for too long. Give yourself permission to proceed and concentrate on your well-being.

Distance yourself: If necessary, create some space from the person you have emotions for if being near them is making you feel really uncomfortable. This doesn't entail fully shutting people off; rather, it means striking a balance that enables you to safeguard your emotional wellbeing.

Focus on self improvement: Channel your energy towards personal development and self-improvement by concentrating on it. Take part in enjoyable activities, follow your hobbies, and make an investment in your own growth. This might help you improve your confidence and divert your attention from the unrequited crush.

Ask for help from friends and family: Speak with dependable friends or family members who can listen to you out and give support. Sharing your emotions with a trustworthy person might make you feel less emotionally burdened and provide you new insight.

Avoid excess rumination: While it's normal to think about the person you have a crush on, try to refrain from obsessively overanalyzing their behaviour or possible consequences. The healing process might be slowed down by thinking about "what ifs" and running over situations again in your head.

Open up to new possibilities: Keep your mind and heart open to new experiences and prospective relationships. Be receptive to new opportunities. Recognise that the future holds many chances for love and fulfilling connections. Accepting new possibilities may aid in your progress and pleasure.

Dealing with unrequited crushes requires tolerance, self-compassion and time. Concentrate on your own development and wellbeing and have faith that you will eventually recover and find happiness.

Expressing Feelings And Communication Challenges

A difficult and emotional situation is having an unrequited crush. In such circumstances, it is normal to experience a range of emotions and encounter communication difficulties. Here are some strategies for expressing your emotions and overcoming communication barriers after an unrequited crush:

Make time for yourself: Give yourself time to recover and space to digest your feelings. Recognise that feeling dissatisfied, unhappy, or even furious is common. Allow yourself to feel these feelings without holding them against yourself.

Journaling: Putting your feelings and ideas down on paper may be therapeutic. It enables you to openly express your emotions and obtain understanding of your experience. Additionally, keeping a journal might help you see trends or acquire understanding of your own development.

Consider the lessons you've learnt and how you can use this experience to advance yourself. Think about what this unrequited infatuation has taught you about yourself, your ambitions and your limits. You may handle relationships more skillfully in the future by thinking back on these lessons.

Talk to the individual *(if appropriate)*: If you feel comfortable and think it would be beneficial, you may think about having a frank discussion with the person you formerly harboured feelings for. Nevertheless, it's critical to control your expectations and be ready for a range of outcomes. It's important to respect their sentiments and limits since they may not feel the same way as you do.

Focus on taking care of yourself by doing things that make you happy and advance your goals. Engage in hobbies, physical activity, quality time with loved ones and self-care practices that encourage self-compassion and healing to look after your physical and emotional wellbeing.

Acceptance and letting go: Recognise that you cannot dictate how someone else feels or force them to feel the same way. A crucial step in the healing process is acceptance. You may explore new options and advance by letting go of attachment to a certain result.

TRANSITIONING FROM A CRUSH TO A GENUINE CONNECTION OR FRIENDSHIP

A natural transition from having a crush on someone to developing a sincere relationship or friendship with them might occur. Whether it results in a more profound connection or just a platonic friendship, it demands patience, honest communication and a readiness to accept the conclusion.

You may take the following actions to ease the transition:

Evaluate your sentiments: Think about your feelings and decide whether you really want to become friends with this person, even if love feelings are not shared. Verify that you are at ease with the notion of continuing to be friends without any hopes of finding love.

Give yourself space: If your crush is dominating the majority of your thoughts, give yourself some space and concentrate on other areas of your life. Take part in activities, get out with friends, and spend money on yourself. Your perspective will improve as a result, and the intensity of your emotions will also lessen.

Establish open communication: Open the lines of contact by talking to the individual whenever you feel ready and expressing your intention to form a close relationship or significant connection. Express your emotions openly while highlighting how much you appreciate their presence in your life and how you'd want to know them better.

Focus on common interest: Emphasise shared interests or find common interests, hobbies, things to discuss that may work as the basis for your friendship. Together, take part in these activities and look for chances to socialise in a platonic setting.

Set Boundaries: Clearly defined limits must be established in order to prevent any misconceptions or possible discomfort. Make sure that both sides are clear about your objectives and the kind of connection you are seeking.

Be patient and understanding: Remember that changing from a crush to a friend takes time and may not happen right away. Give the other person room to analyse their emotions as well as their decisions and respect their sentiments. Keep them from being forced into a relationship that they may not be interested in.

Embrace the outcome: Recognise that the other person may not share your desire for friendship and that's alright. It's important to respect their choice and graciously accept their answer. Focus on developing that relationship and having fun together if they're receptive to friendship.

MOVING ON AND THE ROLE OF TIME IN RESOLVING CRUSHES

It may be difficult to get beyond a crush and how time affects crushes might differ from person to person. Even if time by itself doesn't magically make sentiments go away, it often aids in recovery and perspective-finding.

Here are a few ways that passing time might affect how crushes end:

Emotional distance: You could inadvertently begin to become emotionally distant from your crush as time goes on. This distance may help you see the other person more objectively, enabling you to identify their shortcomings and areas of compatibility that you may have first missed.

Clarity and perspective: As time goes on, you could become more aware of the dynamics of your emotions and your infatuation. When you acquire experience and think back on a scenario, you could realise that the truth doesn't match your early thoughts of a crush since it was based on idealised or one-sided notions.

Focus on personal development: Time may provide a chance for introspection and personal development. Focusing on yourself instead of the crush may be achieved by doing things you like, working towards your objectives and making investments in yourself. Building self-assurance and resilience via this process might make it simpler to go on.

As time passes, you can come across new friends, opportunities/acquaintances and prospective love interests. Your horizons may be expanded by making new contacts and this might also provide chances for new relationships or crushes to emerge. This may help you focus on something else and speed up your recovery by taking your mind off your ex.

Every person's crushes resolve differently. Others could benefit from actively working through their feelings or from getting assistance from friends, family or a therapist, while other people may find that time alone is sufficient to help them move on.

HANDLING REJECTION AND UNDERSTANDING PERSONAL AGENCY

Especially when you have a crush on someone, dealing with rejection may be difficult. In such circumstances, it's normal to experience disappointment, hurt or even discouragement. Rejection is a fact of life and how you respond to it may have a significant influence on your mental health. Here are some pointers on how to deal with rejection and comprehend personal agency:

Recognise and deal with your emotions. Feeling a variety of emotions, such as melancholy, annoyance or self-doubt, is perfectly acceptable. Give yourself time to absorb these feelings after allowing yourself to go through them. Speak with a dependable friend or relative who is able to listen and provide assistance.

Remember not to take it personally. Your value as a person is not determined by someone else's choice to reject you. It's crucial to keep your self-esteem independent of rejection. Many of the possible reasons why someone may not feel the same way about you may have nothing to do with you.

Consider the situation and give it some thought, try to get some perspective. Examine if there were any clues or hints that the individual wasn't romantically interested in you. You may go on and accept the rejection if you are aware of these indications.

Put your attention on your own development. Make use of this experience to further your development. Spend some time on your interests, pastimes and personal growth. Taking part in activities that make you happy and fulfilled might assist to increase your self-worth and confidence.

Keep things in perspective and keep in mind that falling in love is just one part of your life. It's critical to keep a bigger picture in mind and avoid letting rejection overwhelm other aspects of your life, such as friendships, interests and objectives. Put your energy into things that make you happy and give you a feeling of purpose.

Self-care is a virtue. Look after your physical and emotional needs. Take part in things that make you feel good, such as working out, meditating, spending time in nature or exploring your creative side. You may develop resilience and a good outlook by taking care of yourself.

Although rejection might be demoralising, it's crucial to remember that you have control over your own life and decisions. Although you have no control over how another person feels or behaves, you do have power over how you react and proceed. Accept your own agency and concentrate on building a satisfying life that is consistent with your beliefs and aspirations.

Keep in mind that everyone encounters rejection at some time in life since it is a normal aspect of existence.

IMPACT OF SOCIAL MEDIA ON CRUSHES AND ONLINE BEHAVIOUR

Crushes and online behaviour have been significantly impacted by social media, changing how individuals express their emotions, engage with others and see relationships. Some of the main consequences are as follows:

Greater visibility and accessibility: Social media platforms provide a setting where people may quickly interact with others, including crushes. In order to communicate with one another, users may follow, like, comment, and send direct messages to one another. This improved accessibility could result in more frequent contacts and more exposure to the world of a crush.

Social media promotes users to curate and exhibit idealised versions of themselves, which enhances self-presentation and image management. People often pick out and accentuate the most alluring elements of their life, generating a "highlight reel" that may not exactly represent reality. As people try to look more alluring or faultless online, they project an idealised image of themselves onto their crushes, which may have an impact on crushes.

Increased propensity for stalking: Thanks to social media, individuals may learn more about the people they like without really speaking to them. This accessibility may encourage more online stalking behaviours including skimming through their postings, looking at their images, and keeping tabs on their whereabouts. People could feel more inclined to look into and keep track of their crushes' internet activities, perhaps going too far and violating their crushes' privacy.

False intimacy may be engendered: The digital world has the potential to engender a false intimacy or closeness. Based on the information given online, people could believe they know their crushes better than they really do. Despite having little to no real–life engagement, this appearance of proximity might make people feel more emotionally involved in the crushes they have.

Jealousy and sentiments of social comparison may be brought on by the carefully regulated nature of social media. Observing a crush socialise or display elements of their life might cause comparisons and unfavourable feelings. Furthermore, the appearance of beautiful or seductive remarks made by other users might make you feel more insecure and envious.

Unfortunately, social media may serve as a forum for cyberbullying and online abuse, which can negatively affect people's crush experiences. Negative remarks, rumours or spiteful behaviour may lead to emotional pain, which can harm relationships and one's sense of self.

Reduced face-to-face communication: As digital communication becomes more important, face-to-face conversation may decline in favour of online communication. Because online conversations can lack the delicacy and depth of interactions in person, this change may make it more difficult to forge meaningful connections and relationships.

It's vital to remember that depending on the person and their use habits, the effect of social media on crushes and online behaviour might change. Social media may help people connect and provide them a place to express themselves, but it also has significant drawbacks and hazards. Effectively handling the impact of social media on crushes requires finding a balance between online and offline connections, establishing boundaries and maintaining a healthy sense of self-worth.

IMPACT ON CURRENT ROMANTIC RELATIONSHIPS

Depending on how they are managed, crushes may affect ongoing romantic relationships in a variety of ways. Here are a few possible outcomes:

Emotional turmoil: If one or both spouses start dating someone else outside of the partnership, it might cause emotional distress for everyone. Guilt, perplexity and even jealousy-based emotions might surface, straining the connection that already exists.

Reduced satisfaction: Having a crush might make you feel unsatisfied in your present relationship. When a person has a crush, they may begin to compare their spouse to the object of their admiration, which may leave them feeling let down or that their partner doesn't measure up.

Distraction and detachment: When someone has a crush, their spouse and the person they are crushing on may compete for their thoughts and attention. As their attention switches to the crush, this may result in a decline in emotional connection and participation in the existing relationship.

Risk of adultery: If limits are breached, a crush sometimes turns into an emotional or physical infidelity. It may seriously undermine trust and cause the present relationship to end if one or both parties act on their emotions or behave inappropriately around the person they have a crush on.

Opportunity for development and communication: On the other side, crushes may also provide a chance for relationship development. It may be an opportunity for the parties to speak candidly and freely about their thoughts, aspirations and any underlying problems they may be dealing with. Couples may deepen their relationship and create coping mechanisms by discussing these feelings together.

Rediscovery of attraction: Having a crush on someone when not in a relationship might sometimes make people remember the traits they once found attractive in their spouse. It could act as a wake-up call, inspiring them to respect and enjoy their existing union even more, resulting in a rekindled feeling of commitment.

COMPARISON AND IDEALISATION OF CRUSHES OVER PARTNERS

It's arbitrary to compare crushes and partners since it varies on each person's interests, situation and kind of relationship. I can, however, provide some basic comparisons and ideas to keep in mind while choosing crushes over partners:

- Crushes often cause initial exhilaration and attraction because of their freshness and unfamiliarity. They may look more tempting than a long-term spouse with whom you may have established a more comfortable routine due to this first spark.

- Crushes are often idealised since they mostly reside in our minds. We often project our aspirations and dreams onto them, resulting in an idealised image that may not accurately represent their genuine character or level of compatibility as a relationship. Partners, on the other hand, have had experience in real-life circumstances, making it possible to have a more accurate grasp of their strengths and shortcomings.

- ***Absence of faults:*** Because crushes are often witnessed from a distance or via brief contacts, it is simpler to ignore their faults and shortcomings. But with partners, we experience their presence in our lives in a more nuanced way, and we learn more about their peculiarities, frailties, and weaknesses.

- **Depth of Connection:** Although a crush may elicit strong emotions, it often falls short of the emotional and intellectual depth of connection that can arise in a committed relationship. Partners have the opportunity to get to know you better over time, share similar experiences, and provide a stronger basis for a long-term union.

- ***Long-Term Compatibility:*** Although first crushes may appear ideal, long-term compatibility is crucial for a successful relationship. A greater degree of commitment, similar values, common objectives, and the capacity to overcome obstacles are all characteristics of partnerships that may not be present in a crush.

Idealizing crushes over couples can stem from excitement for new experiences, but it's crucial to treat these emotions mindfully and consider the realities of a committed relationship. To manage these emotions, be honest with your partner and be aware of your own wants and expectations.

JEALOUSY AND INSECURITY IN RELATIONSHIPS DUE TO CRUSHES

Common feelings that might develop because of a variety of factors, including crushes, include jealousy and insecurity in relationships. For the sake of preserving a solid and reliable relationship, it's essential to face these emotions and manage them in a healthy way. Here are some ideas for overcoming the resentment and uneasiness brought on by crushes:

Communicate openly and honestly with your spouse. Avoid making accusations or engaging in conflict. Let your spouse know your worries and apprehensions so they can appreciate them. Open communication promotes understanding and trust.

Self-analysis: Give yourself some time to consider your own feelings and anxieties. Determine the underlying reasons behind your jealousy or insecurity. Are there any unresolved problems from the past that could be causing these feelings? You can articulate your requirements more clearly if you have a deeper understanding of yourself.

Evaluate the relationship: Conduct an unbiased assessment of your connection. Take into account the degree of commitment, trust, and communication you have with your spouse. Recognise that just because you have a crush on someone doesn't imply your spouse no longer cares about you. Concentrate on your relationship's positive aspects and the reasons you two chose to be together.

Establish clear limits with your relationship by talking about them. Boundaries provide both parties a feeling of security and give them direction. Discuss your respective comfort zones for interacting with people, especially crushes.

Building self-confidence: Put effort into enhancing your sense of confidence and self-worth. Pursue personal objectives and engage in things that make you feel good about yourself. Feelings of insecurity may be reduced by developing self-assurance.

Maintain a support system: Ask for help from dependable family members or friends who can give insight and direction. Speaking with someone apart from the relationship might provide insightful advice and comfort.

Remember to stay in the moment and that a crush does not always mean the end of your relationship. Keep your focus on the present and be grateful for the benefits of your existing connection. Focus your efforts on fortifying your relationship and fostering your partner's connection.

Consider seeking the advice of a couples therapist or a mental health professional if necessary if emotions of jealousy and insecurity continue to negatively affect your well-being and the relationship. They may provide direction and assistance that is catered to your particular circumstance.

It's important to keep in mind that jealousy and insecurity are normal human feelings, but how you choose to handle them is very important. To keep a relationship strong and flourishing, open communication, introspection and understanding are essential.

DIFFERENT CULTURAL ATTITUDES AND EXPRESSIONS OF CRUSHES

Here are some examples of various cultural viewpoints and crush expressions:

Western cultures, such as those of the US and Western Europe:

Open expression: People often openly express their crushes by telling the person they are interested in how they feel. This is widespread in many Western cultures. Western societies often have a dating culture in which people go out on dates to get to know one another romantically. Dinner dates, movie dates, and other social events are examples of dating-related activities. Asian Cultures (like South Korea and Japan):

Shyness and indirectness: People may have a propensity to be more reticent and taciturn while expressing their crushes in various Asian cultures. They could use subdued gestures, hints or non-verbal indicators to convey their sentiments.

Arranged marriages and matchmaking: In certain Asian
societies, the idea of matchmakers choosing
prospective couples is still widely used. It may be
necessary to enlist the assistance of relatives or
matchmakers in order to express a crush.

Cultures of the Middle East:

Traditional courting: Traditional courtship traditions
may still be practised in Middle Eastern societies. There
may be a higher focus on family engagement in the love
process, and confessing a crush may include asking the
person's family for permission or acceptance.

Respect and modesty: Many Middle Eastern civilizations
place a great priority on modesty and respect.
Maintaining a certain amount of formality and abiding
by cultural conventions around gender interaction may
be necessary while confessing a crush.

Cultures of Latin America:

Passionate expression and flirtation: In many Latin American cultures, flirting is often seen as an expressive and amusing method to convey interest. There could be more touching, emotional movements, and emphasis on expressing emotions.

Serenades and public displays of passion: In various Latin American cultures, people may show their crushes how they really feel by making romantic gestures like serenades or outward displays of devotion. Grand gestures, which may entail outward shows of devotion, are often seen as romantic.

It's important to remember that these are broad generalisations and that even within the same culture, sentiments and crush manifestations may differ widely. Furthermore, cultural views may change throughout time since they are not constant.

MEDIA AND POPULAR CULTURE'S INFLUENCE ON CRUSHES

Crushes and love interests are surely greatly influenced by the media and popular culture. They may affect our perceptions and preferences in the following ways:

Idealised portrayals: Idealised romantic relationships and characters are often shown in films, television programmes, and novels. These representations may provide a benchmark or model for what is seen desirable or alluring. People who exhibit these idealised qualities, such as physical attractiveness, charisma, confidence, or certain personality characteristics, may inspire crushes.

Celebrity crushes: Popular culture is greatly influenced by celebrities, such as actors, singers, sports, and other prominent people. Many individuals get crushes on celebrities, often because they are inspired by their abilities, looks, or imagined way of life. The widespread coverage of celebrities' lives in the media makes them more approachable and fosters a feeling of familiarity that may lead to crushes.

Social media: Sites like Instagram, TikTok and YouTube provide a window into the worlds of content producers and influencers. These people often develop personalities or carefully produced pictures that might be alluring or enticing to their followers. Based on these people's online personas and the imagined closeness or connection that is fostered via social media interactions, people could start to develop crushes on them.

Romantic plots and storylines: Romantic plots and storylines may arouse feelings and imaginations in viewers and readers of films, television programmes, and novels. These stories often depict idealised relationships, evoking a yearning or desire for such experiences. The romantic dynamics they find intriguing may cause viewers to develop crushes on fictitious characters or transfer their wants onto real-life people.

Peer pressure and trends: The media and popular culture affect society norms and trends. Crushes may be affected by what is now fashionable or popular. People may develop crushes on certain artists, musicians or characters as a result of peer pressure or media attention, for instance, if they get a lot of attention or are widely admired.

CROSS-CULTURAL COMPARISONS OF CRUSH EXPERIENCES

Due to cultural conventions, morals and social expectations, crush experiences may range greatly across countries. It's difficult to present a comprehensive list of cross-cultural comparisons, but I can talk about some broad trends. Keep in mind that while people's experiences may still vary within a particular cultural setting, these insights might not be applicable to every person within a culture.

Expression of feelings: People may show their love interest or desire for someone they have a crush on more directly and openly in different cultures. Direct communication or even public demonstrations of love might be part of this. People in different cultures could be more reserved and prefer to convey their sentiments subtly or indirectly, allowing the other person to infer what they mean.

Gender roles and expectations: Crushes may be influenced by different cultural expectations about gender roles and behaviours. There may be more conventional expectations in certain cultures, where males are often expected to make the first move and begin romantic relationships. Other cultures, on the other hand, could support gender equality and permit more egalitarian methods of expressing love desire.

Cultural standards for dating: Crush experiences might be influenced by cultural standards for dating. According to certain cultures, courting may be governed by particular customs or rituals, such as formal introductions, parental participation or planned unions. These traditions may have an effect on how people approach their crushes and handle romantic relationships.

Influence of family and community: Cultural norms that place a high priority on close family and community relationships may have an impact on crushes. In certain cultures, the acceptance and views of one's family or the wider community may have a big impact on love relationships. This may contribute to the pressure people feel while expressing their emotions or selecting a mate.

Attitudes regarding public displays of affection *(PDA)*: Crush experiences may be influenced by cultural attitudes about PDA. Public displays of romantic or physical love may be more acceptable or even encouraged in different cultures. However, similar behaviour could be frowned upon or seen inappropriately in other cultures, causing people to be more subdued about their crushes in public places.

Social media and technology's role: Crush experiences may be affected differently by social media and technology in different cultural contexts. Online dating sites and apps may be widely accepted and utilised as resources for discovering and expressing love interest in various societies. Other cultures, on the other hand, can still largely depend on conventional means of finding prospective partners or be sceptical about online connections.

It's important to understand that these are only generalisations and that cultures may differ significantly from one another. People within a culture may have a variety of viewpoints and experiences when it comes to crushes and love relationships since cultures are not monolithic.

CONCLUSION

Recap Of Key Points Regarding Crushes

An extreme love attraction or infatuation for someone is referred to as a crush. It entails a great yearning for intimacy and a heightened interest in the person's existence.

Crushes often result in a variety of sensations, such as butterflies in the stomach, daydreaming, an elevated heart rate, trepidation and an all-around feeling of excitement being near or thinking about the person.

Frequently thinking about someone, wanting to spend more time with them, being possessive or jealous, feeling awkward or timid around them and finding them very beautiful are some typical indications that you have a crush on them.

Crushes are impacted by hormonal changes in the body, especially during adolescence when people encounter higher amounts of hormones like oestrogen and testosterone, which cause strong sensations of desire.

Crushes may vary in strength and length. They can also be transient. They could be transient, perhaps lasting a few days or weeks or they might last for weeks, months or even years. It's vital to remember that not all first impressions lead to meaningful, lasting relationships.

Idealisation: When you have a crush, it's normal to idealise the other person and concentrate on their favourable traits, often ignoring any shortcomings or undesirable characteristics. The strength of the sentiments may be influenced by this idealisation.

Crushes often entail thinking and fantasising about romantic possibilities or potential interactions with the other person. These imaginations might provide a momentary escape and a feeling of joy.

One-sided Nature: Sometimes, crushes are one-sided, meaning that the other person does not feel the same way about you. Disappointment, despair or rejection may result from this.

Crushes are often kept private, particularly if one worries about being rejected or embarrassed. When sentiments are expressed to reliable confidantes, they may provide support and guidance.

Communication is crucial for the growth of a possible love connection, especially if there are shared sentiments between the two parties. Clarifying aims and fostering a stronger relationship may both be facilitated by sharing sentiments.

Though they may be thrilling and delightful, it's crucial to have a balanced viewpoint and respect other people's limits and permission. Have in mind that crushes are a normal aspect of the human experience.

Encouragement For A Balanced Approach To Crushes In Life

Crushes are a common occurrence in life, therefore it's important to address them rationally.

Here are some uplifting ideas to keep your perspective in check:

It's OK to have crushes and to feel attracted to someone; embrace your emotions. Experience those feelings and accept them without passing judgement. It is a characteristic of being human.

Remember to keep things in perspective: A crush is just a crush. Your value or pleasure are not determined by it. Remember that it often stems from idealised beliefs and incomplete information about the other person.

Instead of dwelling on your crush, put your attention on yourself and your personal progress. Follow your interests, engage in enjoyable activities and make an investment in your personal development. This will not only make you a better version of yourself, but it will also serve as a useful diversion.

If the person you're crushing on is someone you already know, value your relationship with them. Instead of concentrating primarily on potential romantic entanglements, cultivate a real bond and enjoy each other's presence. Genuine friendships are priceless and may provide a great deal of support and satisfaction.

Remind yourself that there are many possible mates out there even if it's normal to be attracted to someone. Remain open to new relationships and chances and avoid becoming fixated on a particular individual. You might make unanticipated connections and meet someone who actually enhances your life.

Make self-care a priority by attending to your mental and physical well-being. Take care of your physical, mental and emotional needs. Spend time with loved ones, partake in happy-making activities and engage in self-compassion exercises. Keep in mind that the result of a crush shouldn't determine your level of enjoyment in any way.

Practise appreciation by acknowledging the good things in your life other than your crush. Pay attention to your successes, your connections, and the enjoyable experiences you have. Developing thankfulness may keep you grounded and change your viewpoint.

Healthy emphasis on your own development and happiness is essential to a balanced attitude to crushes. You'll design a trip that is more meaningful and well-rounded if you value yourself and take care of other facets of your life.

EPILOGUE

"Friends, embrace new connections, celebrate shared affection and have faith that the right person will come along at the right time. Cultivating a crush is ok, whether mutual or unrequited and move forward with grace and optimism. Remember, the most important crush is the one you have on yourself".

Also have a look at our book, which will aid you in your quest for self-love:

Denial Is OK